VOLCANOLOGIST

KEVIN CUNNINGHAM

CHERRY LAKE
Publishing

Published in the United States of America by Cherry Lake Publishing
Ann Arbor, Michigan
www.cherrylakepublishing.com

Content Adviser: Wendy Stovall, researcher for the U.S. Geological Survey
Reading Adviser: Marla Conn, ReadAbility, Inc.

Photo Credits: ©Elena Kalistratova/Shutterstock Images, cover, 1, 11; © ZU_09/iStockphoto, 5; © Flory/iStockphoto, 6; © National Geographic Image Collection/Alamy, 8; HVO-USGS, 13; USGS, 14, 6, 24, 25, 26; © Johnny Wagner/ZUMA Press/Newscom, 16; © Lexschmidt | Dreamstime.com - Hikers On Volcano Etna Photo; © Wollertz/Shutterstock Images, 20; © TomKli/Shutterstock Images, 23; © Maridav/Shutterstock Images, 28

Library of Congress Cataloging-in-Publication Data

Cunningham, Kevin, 1966–author.
  Volcanologist/Kevin Cunningham.
    pages cm.—(Cool STEAM careers)
  Summary: "Readers will learn what it takes to succeed as a volcanologist. The book also explains the necessary educational steps, useful character traits, potential hazards, and daily job tasks related to this career. Sidebars include thought-provoking trivia. Questions in the backmatter ask for text-dependent analysis. Photos, a glossary, and additional resources are included."—Provided by publisher.
  Audience: Ages 8–12
  Audience: Grades 4 to 6
  Includes bibliographical references and index.
  ISBN 978-1-63362-568-6 (hardcover)—ISBN 978-1-63362-658-4 (pbk.)—ISBN 978-1-63362-748-2 (pdf)—ISBN 978-1-63362-838-0 (ebook)
  1. Volcanologists–Juvenile literature. 2. Volcanological research—Juvenile literature. 3. Geology—Vocational guidance—Juvenile literature. 4. Volcanoes—Juvenile literature. I. Title. II. Series: 21st century skills library. Cool STEAM careers.

  QE34.C86 2015
  551.21023—dc23
                            2015005368

Cherry Lake Publishing would like to acknowledge the work of The Partnership for 21st Century Skills. Please visit www.p21.org for more information.

Printed in the United States of America
Corporate Graphics

ABOUT THE AUTHOR

Kevin Cunningham is the author of 60 books, including a series on diseases in history and books in Cherry Lake's Global Products series. He lives near Chicago, Illinois.

TABLE OF CONTENTS

STEAM is the acronym for Science, Technology, Engineering, Arts, and Mathematics. In this book, you will read about how each of these study areas is connected to a career in volcanology.

CHAPTER 1

A Deadly Day in Pompeii

Heat baked the Roman resort town of Pompeii on August 24, 79 CE. The sea was a mile to the west. Not much father to the north loomed Vesuvius. The volcano rumbled and smoked, just as it had for days.

A Roman teen named Pliny was living in the popular resort town with Pliny the Elder, his uncle and adopted father. He wondered if an earthquake was on the way. A quake had badly damaged Pompeii 15 years earlier.

Suddenly columns of ash rose on the mountainside. The houses in Pompeii shook. Vesuvius erupted,

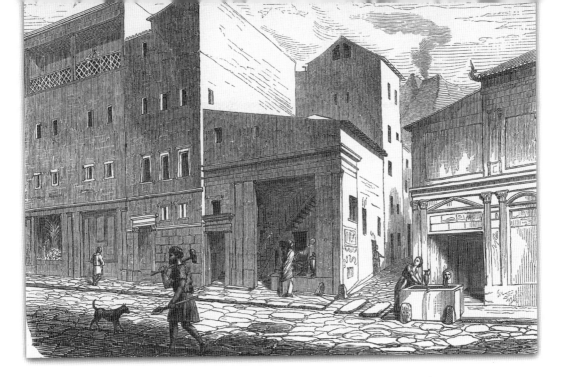

Mount Vesuvius had occasional small clouds of ash and steam coming from its summit in the days before the violent eruption.

blowing tons of rock into the sky and onto Pompeii. Choking light gray ash filled the air. Years later, the younger Pliny remembered how people reacted:

As a protection against falling objects they put pillows on their heads tied down with cloths. There was daylight by this time, but they were still in darkness, blacker and denser than any ordinary night, which they relieved by lighting torches and various kinds of lamp. My uncle decided to go down to the shore and investigate on the spot the possibility of any escape by sea, but he found the waves still wild and dangerous.

Archaeologists have been able to learn a lot from the eruption of Mount Vesuvius by studying the remains of Pompeii.

Ash and **fumes** caused Pliny the Elder to collapse and die. Thirteen to 21 feet (4 to 6.4 meters) of ash and rock buried the town around him.

It is unknown how many of Pompeii's estimated 20,000 citizens died during the eruption. But no one ever lived in the town again. Pompeii vanished from history for almost 1,700 years. In 1748, an engineer named Rocque Joaquin de Alcubierre began digging it out. Since then, millions of tourists have visited the

ruins, to wonder at ancient Roman life and the immense
power of volcanoes.

THINK ABOUT ENGINEERING

*Careless digging destroyed many of Pompeii's buildings and
artworks. In 1863, archaeologist Giuseppe Fiorelli found a way to
save the town's priceless treasures. Before Fiorelli, teams of
workers dug a trench and worked from the bottom up, which
damaged many structures. Fiorelli ordered his people to start at
the top and go slowly, layer by layer, working from the surface
toward the bottom. Like many innovators, Fiorelli suffered for
trying to bring about change. The King of Naples disagreed with
his new methods and sentenced him to time in prison.*

BECOMING A VOLCANOLOGIST

Ancient people knew little about how volcanoes worked. Today, experts called volcanologists help us understand these natural wonders. Volcanologists spend their entire careers studying the always fascinating, sometimes dangerous mountains that blast searing-hot ash, rock, and gas into the sky and create river-like **lava** flows that pour out over the land.

Would-be volcanologists pack math and science into their list of classes in high school. That list includes algebra, geometry, physics, and chemistry. Computer

To do their jobs, volcanologists must go into the heart of danger, sometimes working on active volcanoes.

skills, including knowledge of a programming language, are also important.

In college, a volcanology student takes even more math, science, and computing. Not surprisingly, many study geology, the science of the earth and how it works. Others start out in engineering or geography. A university with a geology program will probably offer volcanology classes. Students at places like the University of Hawaii even get to take field trips to nearby volcanoes. Often, students continue their studies beyond the basic four-year education.

Have a sense of adventure? Like getting your hands dirty outside? Don't mind sleeping in a tent? Then you're ready to go into the field. Studying volcanology sometimes means going to, and staying at, volcanoes for months at a time. Knowing how to live in the outdoors—whether you learned it in scouting, Outward

THINK ABOUT SCIENCE

By using digital cameras and the Global Positioning System (GPS), volcanologists can detect buildup of volcanic fluid or other material within the mountain. A bulge means activity below the surface. Activity means an eruption could be in the works. In 1991, a volcano in the Philippines named Mount Pinatubo began to rumble. Volcanologists were worried about the 1 million people in the area and studied what was happening. They found evidence of activity and warned people to leave. Although more than 700 people died due to the eruption, tens of thousands of others survived, thanks to volcanologists' warnings.

Bound, or another kind of program—comes in handy. Being in good physical shape is a must. The air around active volcanoes gets smelly and hot. There's a lot of climbing, lifting, and digging, and scrambling over rocks. A sudden eruption may even force a volcanology team to run for safety.

Mount Tungurahua, in Ecuador, erupts regularly.

CHAPTER 3

ON THE JOB

Life as a professional volcanologist means mixing adventure, detective work, and careful scientific study. Volcanologists usually hold jobs with one of four kinds of institutions.

Many work for colleges and universities. There, they do research. Some also teach as professors. There are over 30 volcanology programs in American universities. Many of them are based on the West Coast, but other states across the country offer classes in volcanology as well.

Government agencies like the United States

This volcanologist is taking a sample of active lava from Kīlauea Volcano, in Hawaii.

Geological Survey (USGS) employ volcanologists. USGS volcanologists also do research, but most importantly, they keep watch on volcanoes, especially dangerous ones, and issue warnings if necessary. They also add their knowledge to emergency plans for towns and cities near the mountain. If the volcano erupts, these plans help police, fire, and other departments get people out of harm's way.

Volcanologists who work at an **observatory** usually study one or more volcanoes in an area. In the United

This device is called a "spider." It transmits data from a seismometer to an observatory.

States, these places are all staffed by USGS volcanologists. Other countries have their own observatories that are run by local universities and government agencies.

Finally, volcanologists from around the world work for research organizations. One is the International Association of Volcanology and Chemistry of the Earth's Interior, which participates in scientific projects with other groups.

Volcanologists use special tools to collect information, or **data**. Digital cameras and GPS instruments are part of the tool kit. Volcanologists also rely on **seismometers**. These machines measure and record movements in the ground, which are called earthquakes. Volcanologists can use the measurements to learn if the volcano is doing what it normally does, calming down, or becoming more active.

Magma, the molten rock that exists inside a volcano, offers volcanologists other kinds of data. After magma

Seismometers can help volcanologists predict what a volcano is likely to do next.

Lava can damage the vegetation in the path of its flow.

erupts from the **vent** on the volcano's surface, it is called lava. By studying lava when it cools, volcanologists learn about the types of rock inside the volcano. Tests also show the amount of gas in the magma. Gas offers important clues to how powerful the next eruption will be.

Once a volcano goes quiet, volcanologists gather rocks and other materials to study. Knowing how a volcano behaved throughout its history is important for understanding what it may do in the future. Volcanologists also take helicopter flights to places where instruments (like seismometers and GPS) sit on the top or sides of a volcano in order to perform maintenance like changing batteries, fixing solar panels, or collecting data. The volcanology team must collect information and stay alert for signs of another eruption.

THINK ABOUT TECHNOLOGY

*Scientists have been building seismometers since ancient times. The first one was likely built by Zhang Heng around 132 CE. When the earth shook, one of the dragons around the top of his bronze sculpture dropped a ball that landed in a frog's mouth below. Today's seismometers not only detect movements in the earth, they record them. Not long ago, a seismometer showed ground movement on paper (a **seismograph**). A pen connected to the machine drew zigzag lines on the moving piece of paper when the earth moved. Today, a seismometer feeds its data into a computer.*

Volcanoes in Action

Volcanologists study three kinds of volcanoes. Extinct volcanoes no longer erupt. Dormant volcanoes can erupt but have not done so in a long time. Active volcanoes—the kind that can and do erupt—concern volcanologists the most. Of the world's 600 or so active volcanoes, more than 450 sit near or around the edge of the Pacific Ocean, in an upside-down U. Volcanologists call this intense volcanic region the Ring of Fire.

The Ring of Fire sits above where the giant **plates** of the earth's crust meet. In some places, one plate moves

[21ST CENTURY SKILLS LIBRARY]

Mount Etna is Europe's largest active volcano. Its documented eruptions go back more than 2,000 years.

under another. In others, they pull apart or slide past each other. As the plates move, magma is able to form or pool within the crust and eventually erupt through vents.

Fractures, or tears, in the earth's crust allow magma and superheated gas from deep inside to rise and escape. Over hundreds of thousands of years, lava from many eruptions piles up to form a mountain, new shoreline, or even islands. Volcanoes formed Iceland, the Hawaiian Islands, and many other places. In 2013, a volcanic island about 660 feet (201 m) wide rose out of the ocean off the coast of Japan.

A huge volcanic eruption thousands of years ago formed Crater Lake.

Sometimes volcanoes are so big that if a massive amount of magma erupts extremely violently, the top of the volcano will collapse in on itself and form a **caldera**, which is a massive **crater**. At Crater Lake, in Oregon, little remains of Mount Mazama. A huge eruption caused Mazama to blow its top off about 7,600 years ago. Melted snow and rainfall have since formed a deep lake in the collapsed area.

When a volcano erupts, volcanologists place the event into a category. One kind of eruption forms giant, dark clouds of ash and gas (**Plinian**). Another type shoots out chunks of glowing lava like fireworks (Strombolian or Hawaiian).

Volcanologists created the term Plinian eruption in honor of Pliny the Younger of Pompeii. During Plinian events, a volcano explosively erupts a column of ash and gas up to 30 miles (48 kilometers) into the atmosphere, where it spreads out an enormous cloud of ash. The eruptions can also send out waves of super-hot, choking gas that sweep down the mountainside and over the land. Such waves killed many of the thousands who died during the Plinian event at Pompeii in 79 CE.

THINK ABOUT MATH

In 2010, a dormant volcano erupted in Iceland after being quiet for almost 200 years. The flecks of powdery, sharp ash that were shot into the sky might have gummed up jet engines and caused planes to crash. Worried airlines canceled thousands of flights. Soon, mathematicians built computer programs that could keep track of wind speed, the weight of the ash, and other factors. These programs, called **models**, allow airlines and governments to understand what may happen in a future volcanic eruption. The models can help people make plans for the next eruption.

KEEPING WATCH

Mount Rainier looms over Seattle and its 1.5 million people. Tokyo, Japan's capital, sits in the shadow of Mount Fuji. Popocatepetl, near Mexico City, threatens more than 20 million area residents. The people in these places may not worry about the nearby volcanoes. But volcanologists take the threats seriously. History shows the kind of destruction an eruption can unleash.

Volcanoes have destroyed major cities. In May 1902, the crater atop Mount Pelée on the Caribbean island of Martinique collapsed as the mountain shook. Water mixed

Because Mount Rainier may erupt again, people who live nearby are aware of the danger and sometimes practice evacuation drills.

with soil and volcanic **debris** on the mountainside to create a **lahar**, a sort of mud avalanche. The lahar killed 23 people. But the worst was still to come. Early on the morning of May 8, Pelée exploded. A cloud of gas, ash, and rock rolled down the mountainside at over 100 miles per hour (161 km) and hit St. Pierre, Martinique's major city. Of the 28,000 people in St. Pierre, only three survived—one of whom had been underground, in a jail cell. The eruption was so powerful it even destroyed ships anchored offshore.

This device, seen here at Mount St. Helens, measures the ground movement that comes from lahars.

Volcanoes have destroyed whole islands. Krakatau sat in the sea between Sumatra and Java in what is modern-day Indonesia. On August 26, 1883, Krakatau erupted. The next day, the mountain blew itself apart.

The first blast from Krakatau created the loudest noise in recorded history. People 3,000 miles (4,828 km) away thought cannons were going off. At Krakatau, the same kind of waves of hot, suffocating gas that struck Pompeii swept through villages and even killed people 30 miles (48 km) away. Huge **tsunamis** churned up by the event crashed into nearby islands. Hot ash rained down. The shock wave from Krakatau's fourth and final explosion traveled around the earth seven times. At least 36,000 people died. When the smoke cleared, most of the island that Krakatau had sat upon was gone.

Active volcanoes grumble in Alaska and Hawaii, and on the U.S. Pacific coast. The deadliest U.S. eruption in recent history took place in 1980. During the spring of that year, Mount St. Helens in Washington shook and released steam.

Volcanologists with the USGS continue to watch Mount St. Helens with seismometers and other tools.

Government volcanologist David A. Johnston was part of the team that predicted the 1980 Mount St. Helens eruption. He was killed in the eruption.

Volcanologists soon spotted a huge bulge on its north side.

At 8:32 a.m. on May 18, 1980, the bulge blew open. A landslide of gas, steam, and rocks at a temperature of 300 degrees Fahrenheit (149 degrees Celsius) roared down the mountain at hundreds of miles per hour. Tons of snow and ice melted. A river of mud, water, and rock covered the valley below in 640 feet (195 m) of debris. The Plinian ash cloud rained upon people's property more than 900 miles (1,488 km) away. Few people lived near Mount St. Helens. But the eruption still killed 57, including USGS volcanologist David A. Johnston.

Kīlauea, in Hawaii, has been erupting nonstop since 1983. Nearby Mauna Loa has erupted more than 30 times since 1840. The USGS has an observatory nearby to closely study the relatively mild eruptive activity. Tourists also visit Hawaii Volcanoes National Park to see lava flows and **plumes** of volcanic gas. Park rangers suggest the following safety guidelines when visiting the park:

THINK ABOUT ART

Mount Fuji is Japan's tallest mountain. An active volcano, it last erupted in 1707 to 1708. To the Japanese, Fuji represents far more than a volcano. It plays an important role in the country's religion and folklore. Fuji also inspires works of art. Katsushika Hokusai created his world-famous Thirty-Six Views of Mount Fuji between 1826 and 1833. These prints show the mountain from different angles and distances and in different seasons. Thirty-Six Views of Mount Fuji proved so popular that Hokusai added 10 more prints to his series.

- Wear closed-toe shoes to protect your feet and gardening gloves to protect your hands in case you fall on the hot, razor-sharp ground.
- Take lots of water to drink. The air around volcanoes can be very hot.
- Stay away from the deadly cloud of hydrochloric acid where lava flows into the ocean.
- Always stay in the areas marked as safe. Otherwise, you may fall through some thin lava crust.

Volcanologists face challenges like working in dangerous conditions and being under intense pressure during an eruption. Deadly gases and the threat of explosions present dangers found in few other jobs. But working volcanologists express a deep love of their work. Every day, they climb a mountain, analyze material in a laboratory, or sit down at a computer to do a job they enjoy. They get to learn new scientific facts, and their work saves lives. It's no surprise that a person who becomes a volcanologist often sticks with it for good.

Tourists visiting volcanoes need to be careful. These people may be in danger.

THINK ABOUT IT

Go online and find a video of a volcano erupting. Reread chapters 3 and 4. What parts of the volcano can you identify?

Look at a map online and find the volcano closest to where you live. When was the last time it erupted? Is it dormant now, or still active?

Go online to look up activities where you can create your own volcano eruption using common household objects. With the help of an adult, try one at home or at school. Which type of eruption do you create?

Go online to find out more about a famous volcanologist. How did he or she become interested in that field? How does his or her education and training compare to the information in chapters 2 and 3?

LEARN MORE

FURTHER READING

Fradin, Judith, and Dennis Fradin. *Volcano! The Icelandic Eruption of 2010 and Other Hot, Smoky, Fierce, and Fiery Mountains.* Washington, DC: National Geographic for Kids, 2010.

Furgang, Kathy. *Everything Volcanoes and Earthquakes.* Washington, DC: National Geographic for Kids, 2013.

Garbe, Suzanne. *The Worst Volcanic Eruptions of All Time.* North Mankato, MN: Capstone, 2012.

WEB SITES

BBC: The Supervolcano Game—Respond to a Disaster
www.bbc.co.uk/sn/tvradio/programmes/supervolcano/game.shtml
Play this online game that challenges you to get people away from an erupting volcano.

How Volcanoes Work
www.geology.sdsu.edu/how_volcanoes_work/Home.html
This San Diego State University site offers information on all things volcanic.

Mila: Live from Iceland
www.livefromiceland.is/webcams/hekla
Keep watch on Iceland's Mount Hekla volcano with this online Webcam.

GLOSSARY

caldera (kal-DER-uh) a part of a mountain that has collapsed due to a volcanic eruption

crater (KRAY-tur) a bowl-shaped depression at the mouth of a volcano

data (DAY-tuh) factual information for analysis

debris (duh-BREE) scattered remains of something broken or destroyed

fractures (FRAK-churz) breaks or cracks in something

fumes (FYOOMZ) dangerous gases or smoke

lahar (LAH-har) a mud avalanche triggered by a volcanic eruption

lava (LAH-vuh) the hot, liquid rock that pours out of a volcano when it erupts; the rock formed when this liquid has cooled and hardened

magma (MAG-muh) melted rock material under the earth's crust

models (MAH-duhlz) programs created by mathematicians to re-create a natural event

observatory (uhb-ZUR-vuh-tor-ee) a building dedicated to the study of the natural world

plates (PLAYTZ) the flat, rocky, rigid pieces that make up the earth's outer crust

Plinian (PLY-nee-an) a kind of volcanic eruption that sends out lava and throws gas and ash high into the sky

plumes (PLOOMZ) things that have a feathery shape

seismograph (SIZE-muh-graf) the measurements from a seismometer

seismometers (size-MAH-mi-turz) machines that measure movement in the earth

tsunamis (tsoo-NAH-meez) huge ocean waves that travel at high speeds and sometimes hit land

vent (VENT) the opening in a volcano through which smoke and lava escape

INDEX

[21ST CENTURY SKILLS LIBRARY]